Taste of
CHRISTMAS

Traditional Turkey
& Other Classic Holiday Recipes

COOKBOOK

Recipes and Holiday Inspiration

BARBOUR BOOKS
An Imprint of Barbour Publishing, Inc.

Angels from the realms of glory,
Wing your flight o'er all the earth;
Ye who sang Creation's story
Now proclaim Messiah's birth.
Come and worship, come and worship;
Worship Christ, the newborn King.

JAMES MONTGOMERY

Taste of CHRISTMAS

Traditional Turkey
& Other Classic Holiday Recipes

COOKBOOK

Recipes and Holiday Inspiration

© 2014 by Barbour Publishing, Inc.

Written and compiled by MariLee Parrish.

ISBN 978-1-62836-876-5

All scripture quotations are taken from the King James Version of the Bible.

Published by Barbour Books, an imprint of Barbour Publishing, Inc., P.O. Box 719, Uhrichsville, Ohio 44683, www.barbourbooks.com

Our mission is to publish and distribute inspirational products offering exceptional value and biblical encouragement to the masses.

Member of the
Evangelical Christian
Publishers Association

Printed in the United States of America.

 Contents

Christmas is full of memories and favorite holiday traditions. Some traditions are so ingrained in our celebrations that it just wouldn't feel like Christmas without them. This recipe book is full of all of your favorite classic Christmas recipes to keep your traditions alive and strong this holiday season.

Blessings to you and yours,
MariLee Parrish
www.marileeparrish.com

 # Classic Holiday Beverages

*When they saw the star, they rejoiced with exceeding
great joy. And when they were come into the house, they
saw the young child with Mary his mother, and fell down,
and worshipped him: and when they had opened
their treasures, they presented unto him gifts;
gold, and frankincense, and myrrh.*

MATTHEW 2:10–11

Cranberry Christmas Punch

2 cups fresh cranberries
2 cups water

¼ cup sugar
2 cups pineapple juice

Cook cranberries in water until soft. Strain. Add ¼ cup sugar and bring to a boil. Chill. Add pineapple juice just before serving.

Traditional Eggnog

6 eggs, slightly beaten

4 cups whole milk

¼ cup sugar

¼ teaspoon salt

2 cups whipping cream or 1 pint
  vanilla ice cream

Dash nutmeg

Peppermint sticks

In large, heavy saucepan, mix eggs, milk, sugar, and salt. Cook and stir over medium heat until mixture coats a metal spoon. Remove from heat. Fold in whipping cream or ice cream. Pour into punch bowl or pitcher. Cover and refrigerate overnight. Sprinkle each serving with nutmeg. Serve with a peppermint stick.

Grandma's Hot Chocolate

2 ounces unsweetened chocolate

⅓ cup sugar

4 cups whole milk

Dash salt

½ teaspoon vanilla

Marshmallows or whipped cream

Place chocolate, sugar, milk, and salt in medium saucepan over medium-low heat. Stirring constantly, heat until chocolate melts and mixture is well blended. Add vanilla and serve warm. Top with marshmallows or whipped cream.

Cranberry Ginger Punch

1 quart cranberry juice cocktail   1 orange, sliced

1 (6 ounce) can frozen orange juice   Fresh cranberries

2 (16 ounce) bottles ginger ale

Mix all of the liquids together. Garnish with orange slices and fresh cranberries. Serve cold.

Christmas Cheer Punch

1 (3 ounce) package raspberry gelatin

1 cup boiling water

1 (6 ounce) can frozen lemonade

3 cups cold water

1 quart cranberry juice cocktail, chilled

1 (12 ounce) bottle lemon-lime soda, chilled

Festive Ice Cubes (recipe follows)

Dissolve gelatin in boiling water. Add lemonade. Add cold water and cranberry juice cocktail. Add soda and stir. Pour punch into a chilled holiday punch bowl. Add several trays of Festive Ice Cubes.

For a festive touch, freeze cranberries or maraschino cherries in ice cube trays, Bundt cake pans, or gelatin molds, and add them to Christmas punch bowls.

Traditional Wassail

2¼ cups sugar

4 cups water

2 cinnamon sticks

8 whole allspice berries

1 tablespoon whole cloves

1 teaspoon ginger

4 cups orange juice

2 cups lemon juice

8 cups apple juice

In large saucepan, combine sugar and water. Boil for 5 minutes.
Remove from heat. Add cinnamon sticks, allspice berries, cloves, and
ginger. Cover and let stand in warm place for 1 hour. Strain liquid into
large pot, discarding spices. Add juices and quickly bring to a boil.
Remove from heat and serve.

Old-Fashioned Orange Cream

4 cups orange juice (not from concentrate)

3 cinnamon sticks

1 tablespoon vanilla

1 pint vanilla ice cream

Mini marshmallows

Combine orange juice, cinnamon sticks, and vanilla in large saucepan over medium-high heat. Bring mixture to a boil; reduce heat to low. Simmer uncovered for 10 minutes. Remove cinnamon sticks and stir in ice cream. Cook over low heat, stirring constantly, until heated through. Do not allow mixture to boil. Serve with mini marshmallows.

Candy Cane Cocoa

4 cups milk

3 (1 ounce) squares semisweet chocolate, chopped

3 peppermint candy canes, crushed

1 cup whipped cream

4 small peppermint candy canes

In large saucepan, heat milk until hot. Do not boil. Whisk in chocolate and crushed peppermint until melted and smooth. Pour hot cocoa into mugs and top with whipped cream. Serve with a candy cane for stirring.

Slow Cooker Holiday Punch

3 cups orange juice

4 cups apple juice

6 cups cranberry juice cocktail

¾ cup maple syrup

2 teaspoons powdered sugar

1½ teaspoons cinnamon

1 teaspoon nutmeg

1 teaspoon ground cloves

Cinnamon sticks

Combine all ingredients except cinnamon sticks in very large, heavy pan. Bring to a boil and let simmer for 3 minutes. Transfer to slow cooker and keep warm over low heat. Not only is this a warm drink to have handy for company, but it will make your house smell like Christmas, too!

Candy Cane Punch

20 ounces frozen strawberries, unsweetened

1 (46 ounce) can pineapple juice

Lime sherbet

Peppermint candy canes

Place frozen strawberries in blender and puree. In large bowl, combine strawberry puree and pineapple juice. Pour into punch glasses. Top with a spoonful of sherbet and hang a candy cane on the edge of each cup.

Away in a manger, no crib for a bed,
The little Lord Jesus
laid down His sweet head.
The stars in the sky
looked down where He lay,
The little Lord Jesus asleep in the hay.

ANONYMOUS

Cherry Hot Cocoa

3 tablespoons cocoa
¼ cup sugar
4 cups milk

1 teaspoon maraschino cherry juice
(or more to taste)
Whipped cream
Maraschino cherries

Blend cocoa and sugar in small bowl. In medium saucepan, heat milk to scalding. Mix about ⅓ cup of hot milk into cocoa-sugar mixture, then pour cocoa mixture into hot milk in saucepan; stir until well blended. Stir in cherry juice. Top each serving with whipped cream and a cherry.

Hors d'oeuvres and Soups

And she brought forth her firstborn son, and wrapped him in swaddling clothes, and laid him in a manger; because there was no room for them in the inn.

LUKE 2:7

Sausage and Apple Chowder

5 Italian sausage links, hot or mild

5 large potatoes, peeled and cubed

1 tablespoon dried oregano

1 tablespoon parsley

1 tablespoon basil

3 (15 ounce) cans chicken broth

2 tablespoons garlic powder

1 (15 ounce) can diced tomatoes

Water

2 (15 ounce) cans sweet corn

1 cup milk

3 small Red Delicious apples, cored and cubed

Over medium-high heat in Dutch oven, brown sausage links. Drain off fat. Add potatoes, oregano, parsley, and basil. Toss to coat. Add chicken broth, garlic powder, tomatoes, and enough water to cover all ingredients in pot. Bring to a boil; reduce heat and simmer for 1 hour. Add corn and milk and continue cooking, over medium heat, for 15 minutes. Add apples and cook until apples are tender but not mushy. Serve warm.

Festive Eggs

6 hard-cooked eggs, peeled
¼ cup mayonnaise
1 teaspoon mustard
¼ cup shredded cheddar cheese
1 tablespoon fresh parsley
1 tablespoon minced scallions

¼ teaspoon salt
½ teaspoon paprika
¼ teaspoon celery seed
⅛ teaspoon chili powder
Pinch red pepper

Slice each egg in half crosswise. Scrape out yolks; place contents in small bowl. Add mayonnaise and mustard to yolks. Blend together well. Add remaining ingredients and mix well. Spoon 1 tablespoon of mixture into each egg half. Sprinkle lightly with more chili powder if desired.

Herb Cheese Spread

3 tablespoons butter, softened

1 (8 ounce) package cream cheese, softened

1 tablespoon olive oil

2 tablespoons minced sweet onion

2 tablespoons chopped fresh parsley

1 teaspoon garlic powder

½ teaspoon chopped fresh basil

Pinch oregano

Blend butter and cream cheese until smooth. Add remaining ingredients and mix well. Cover and refrigerate. Serve with crackers.

Cranberry Relish

2 large oranges

4 cups fresh cranberries, washed and stemmed

2 red apples, cored but not pared

2 cups water

Peel oranges and reserve half of 1 peel. Chop oranges coarsely. Put cranberries, apples, and reserved peel through the coarse blade of a food chopper, or use a food processor. Add oranges and water; mix well. Refrigerate for at least 2 hours before serving.

Holiday Cabbage Rolls

1 pound lean ground beef
1 pound ground veal
1 pound ground pork
2 eggs
1 cup milk
1 cup fine dry bread crumbs
2 teaspoons salt
2 teaspoons molasses
½ teaspoon ginger

½ teaspoon nutmeg
½ teaspoon allspice
1 medium onion, finely chopped
2 large heads cabbage
1 cup boiling water
½ cup butter
1 cup whole milk
2 tablespoons cornstarch
Toothpicks

Blend meats with eggs, milk, and bread crumbs in large mixing bowl. Stir in salt, molasses, ginger, nutmeg, allspice, and onion. Mix well. Cut out the core of each cabbage. Carefully separate outer 12 leaves of each cabbage and reserve remainder for other uses or discard. Remove thick center vein of each leaf. Drop leaves into boiling water. Cover. Steam for 3 minutes or until soft and bright green.

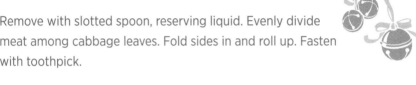

Remove with slotted spoon, reserving liquid. Evenly divide meat among cabbage leaves. Fold sides in and roll up. Fasten with toothpick.

Heat butter in frying pan. Brown cabbage rolls on all sides. Transfer to 3-quart casserole dish as they brown. Mix reserved liquid from boiling leaves with butter and drippings. Pour over filled rolls. Cover and bake at 375 degrees for 1 hour. Remove from oven. Drain off juices into measuring cup. Add milk to equal 2 cups of liquid. Stir in cornstarch. Bring to a boil; cook until thickened. Pour over cabbage rolls. Bake uncovered at 375 degrees for 15 minutes or until browned and heated through.

Old-Fashioned Potato Soup

1 small onion, chopped	1 egg
2 tablespoons butter	½ cup flour
4 medium red potatoes, diced	¼ cup milk
1½ quarts water	½ cup whipping cream
1 teaspoon salt	

Brown onion and butter in saucepan. Add diced potatoes, water, and salt. Bring to a boil and cook until potatoes are soft. Make "rivels" by rubbing egg and flour together. Put in small bowl; add milk. Cut through mixture with 2 forks. Drop "rivels" into boiling potatoes. Stir to prevent packing together. Cook for 5 minutes with pan covered. Add cream. Serve warm.

Classic Winter Chowder

1 cup diced bacon
1 medium onion, chopped fine
4 tablespoons flour
2 cups cubed raw potatoes
2 cups whole kernel corn

2 cups water
2 cups whole milk
1 teaspoon salt
½ teaspoon pepper

Fry bacon until crisp. Remove from pan and set aside. Fry onions in bacon drippings until soft. Stir in flour. Slowly add milk, stirring until thick. Set aside. Cook potatoes and corn in water until potatoes are tender. Add onion gravy to potato mixture. Add bacon and seasonings. Serve hot.

Spicy Chicken Rolls

6 to 8 dinner rolls

2 cups diced cooked chicken

1 cup shredded cheddar cheese

1 (8 ounce) package cream cheese, softened

1 (4 ounce) can chopped green chilies

2 tablespoons chopped green onion

1 teaspoon cumin

1 teaspoon chili powder

¼ teaspoon red pepper

2 tablespoons minced cilantro

Cut small slice off top of each roll and hollow out. Mix together remaining ingredients except cilantro. Fill rolls with mixture and place on cookie sheet. Bake at 375 degrees for 5 to 7 minutes or until golden brown. Sprinkle chicken with cilantro. Garnish with tomato and avocado if desired.

Homemade Meatballs

1½ pounds hamburger
½ cup quick oats
½ cup milk
1 egg
1 small onion, chopped fine

1½ teaspoons salt
½ teaspoon pepper
¼ teaspoon garlic salt
½ teaspoon nutmeg

Combine all ingredients. Form into balls and brown on cookie sheet in 350-degree oven for about 10 minutes. Transfer to slow cooker.

Sauce:
2 cups ketchup
1 tablespoon Worcestershire sauce

1 tablespoon brown sugar
Dash oregano

Combine all sauce ingredients. Pour over meatballs in slow cooker. Cook on high for 1 hour.

Sausage Rolls

18 frozen dinner rolls, thawed

⅛ cup fresh parsley, chopped fine

¼ cup fresh thyme, chopped fine

¼ cup fresh rosemary, chopped fine

1 cup grated Parmesan cheese

½ cup unsalted butter, melted

1 pound mild or spicy sausage, cooked and crumbled

Grease large Bundt pan. Rolls should be thawed but still cold. Flatten each roll into a circle. Combine herbs and cheese in shallow bowl. Place butter in separate shallow bowl. Coat each flattened roll with butter and then with herb mixture. Arrange 6 rolls evenly in prepared pan, covering the bottom. Rolls should overlap. Sprinkle half of cooked sausage over rolls. Repeat with 6 more rolls and remaining sausage. Add last 6 rolls on top to cover sausage. Cover with plastic wrap and let rise until almost doubled. Bake at 350 degrees for 35 minutes. Cover with foil during last 10 minutes of baking. Remove from oven and invert onto serving platter.

Zesty Ham Balls

2 pounds ground ham
2 pounds lean ground beef
1½ cups evaporated milk
2 eggs, slightly beaten
2 cups dry bread crumbs

Sauce:
1 (14 ounce) can tomato soup
1½ cups brown sugar
½ cup vinegar
1 teaspoon prepared mustard

Combine meat, milk, eggs, and bread crumbs. Mix well. Shape into balls and place in shallow baking dish. Combine sauce ingredients and pour over meatballs. Bake at 325 degrees for 1 hour. Baste while cooking.

Vegetable Herb Spread

¾ cup whole milk ricotta cheese

1 stalk celery, chopped fine

2 tablespoons chopped green onions

1 carrot, shredded

2 teaspoons grated Parmesan cheese

2 tablespoons fresh parsley, minced

¾ teaspoon fresh basil, minced

¼ teaspoon oregano, thyme, or marjoram

¼ teaspoon garlic powder

Pepper to taste

Combine all ingredients and blend well. Chill for at least 2 hours. Serve with crackers or inside a large pumpernickel bread bowl.

Prepare meatballs, cookies, and soups a month in advance and freeze. Then when it's time for a celebration you can just thaw and serve. A stress-free way to anticipate the holidays!

Hot Bacon Bean Dip

1 onion, chopped fine

1 teaspoon olive oil

1 (14 ounce) can refried beans with jalapeños

1 pound pepper jack cheese, shredded

½ teaspoon taco seasoning

2 tablespoons fresh cilantro, minced

2 teaspoons garlic powder

4 slices bacon, crisply cooked and crumbled

In medium saucepan, sauté onion in oil over low heat. Add remaining ingredients. Cook over low heat until cheese has melted. Serve with tortilla chips.

Sweet Onion Soup

1 tablespoon butter
1 large sweet onion, sliced thin
½ teaspoon sugar

1 (10 ounce) can beef broth
1¼ cups water
2 tablespoons Worcestershire
   sauce

Melt butter in medium saucepan. Add onion slices and sugar. Cook and stir for 5 to 10 minutes, until lightly browned. Add broth, water, and Worcestershire sauce. Simmer on low for 15 minutes. Top with croutons and swiss and Parmesan cheeses, if desired.

Festive Italian Stromboli

1 (13.8 ounce) tube refrigerated pizza crust

1 tablespoon mustard

1 tablespoon real mayonnaise

¼ pound deli turkey breast

1 cup sliced turkey pepperoni

2 cups shredded mozzarella cheese

On baking sheet, unfold pizza crust and flatten into large rectangle. Spread mustard and mayonnaise over crust. Layer remaining ingredients evenly over crust. Roll up and pinch seam. Cut slit in top for steam to escape. Bake at 400 degrees for 15 minutes or until golden brown. Cut into small slices and serve at holiday get-togethers alongside a dish of pizza sauce.

Bacon Crab Rolls

¼ cup tomato juice

1 egg, beaten

1 (7 ounce) can crabmeat

¼ teaspoon salt

Dash pepper

½ cup Italian bread crumbs

1 tablespoon lemon juice

¼ teaspoon Worcestershire sauce

12 slices bacon, cut in half

Whisk together tomato juice and egg. Add remaining ingredients, except bacon. Mix well. Shape into 24 rolls that are about 2 inches long. Wrap each roll with half slice raw bacon and fasten with toothpick. Broil on baking sheet 5 inches from heat for 10 minutes, turning as needed.

Tomato Basil Bruschetta

3 large tomatoes, diced

1 cup fresh basil

4 tablespoons olive oil

6 cloves garlic, peeled and divided

Kosher salt and fresh ground pepper to taste

2 large baguettes, cut about 1 inch thick to make 36 slices

1½ pounds fresh mozzarella cheese, sliced about ¼ inch thick

Preheat oven to 375 degrees. In food processor, combine tomatoes, basil, olive oil, and 2 cloves of garlic. Process until mixture forms small chunks (like salsa). Season with salt and pepper. Put sliced bread on baking sheet and toast in oven for 3 minutes or until golden brown. Rub garlic cloves on warmed bread, put mozzarella slices on toast, and then place back in oven until melted. Spoon tomato mixture over melted cheese. Serve immediately.

Chipotle Nachos

1 red bell pepper, chopped

1 green bell pepper, chopped

1 small sweet onion, chopped

1 (7 ounce) can chipotle chilies

1 (15 ounce) can pinto beans, drained

1 (14 ounce) can diced tomatoes with basil, garlic, and oregano

¼ cup fresh cilantro, chopped

Sauté pepper and onion in small amount of oil. Remove only 1 chili from can and store remaining in refrigerator. Chop the chili and add it to pepper and onion along with beans and tomatoes. Simmer for 8 to 10 minutes on low. Add cilantro and stir. Serve with tortilla chips. Add chopped avocado, shredded cheese, sour cream, and lettuce if desired.

Sausage Stromboli

1 (13.8 ounce) tube refrigerated pizza crust

1 tablespoon Dijon mustard

1 tablespoon real mayonnaise

½ pound Italian sausage, cooked, cooled, and crumbled

1 (4 ounce) can sliced mushrooms, drained

2 cups shredded mozzarella cheese

On baking sheet, unfold pizza crust and flatten into large rectangle. Spread mustard and mayonnaise over crust. Layer remaining ingredients evenly over crust. Roll up and pinch seam. Cut slit in top for steam to escape. Bake at 400 degrees for 15 minutes or until golden brown.

Crab and Artichoke Spread

1 (14 ounce) can artichoke hearts, chopped

1 (6 ounce) can crabmeat

1 cup grated Parmesan cheese

1 cup mayonnaise

⅛ teaspoon lemon zest

⅛ teaspoon pepper

½ cup Italian bread crumbs

1 tablespoon butter, melted

Chop artichoke hearts with crabmeat. Add cheese, mayo, lemon zest, and pepper. Spoon into baking dish coated with nonstick spray. Mix crumbs with butter and sprinkle over top. Bake at 350 degrees for 20 minutes. Serve with crackers and veggies.

Easy Stuffed Mushrooms

1 pound mushrooms

1 (14 ounce) package stuffing mix, prepared

Remove stems from mushrooms and finely chop. Mix with prepared stuffing. Fill mushroom caps with mixture. Add extra water or butter if mix is too dry. Bake at 350 degrees on greased baking sheet for 15 minutes.

Creamy Crab Chowder

½ cup chopped onion

1 stalk celery, chopped fine

3 tablespoons butter

3 cups whole milk

1 (14 ounce) can cream of potato soup

1 (8 ounce) can creamed corn

1 (6 ounce) can crabmeat

1 cup red potatoes, cooked and chopped

¼ teaspoon salt

Dash thyme

Dash pepper

Sauté onion and celery in butter. Add remaining ingredients. Simmer on low for 15 minutes, stirring frequently.

Merry Minestrone

1 pound ground beef

1 medium onion, chopped

2 (15 ounce) cans tomatoes

4 (10 ounce) cans beef broth

2 cups water

2 teaspoons basil

2 teaspoons oregano

1½ teaspoons garlic salt

1 (20 ounce) package frozen mixed vegetables

1 cup macaroni, uncooked

Brown beef with onion. Add tomatoes, broth, water, spices, and vegetables. Cook for 10 minutes. Add macaroni and cook an additional 7 minutes or until macaroni is tender. Sprinkle with Parmesan cheese if desired.

Tex-Mex Roll-ups

1 (15 ounce) can refried beans

1 cup chunky salsa

1 (15 ounce) can kidney beans,
   rinsed and drained

2 cups cheddar jack cheese

6 (8 inch) corn tortillas

In medium bowl, combine refried beans and salsa. Mix well. Stir in
kidney beans and cheese. Spread on tortillas. Roll up and cut in small
slices for serving.

Freezer Pickles

7 cups small cucumbers, sliced thin

3 medium sweet onions, sliced

2 cups sugar

1 cup vinegar

½ teaspoon celery seed

1 tablespoon salt

Mix all ingredients in large bowl. Refrigerate for 24 hours. Put in containers and freeze for up to 3 months. Makes great gifts, too!

Traditional Cheese Ball

1 (8 ounce) package cream cheese, softened

1 (6 ounce) jar cheddar cheese

1 teaspoon Worcestershire sauce

1 onion, finely grated

6 ounces blue cheese

4 ounces shredded cheddar cheese

½ cup almonds, finely chopped

Combine all ingredients except nuts and form into ball. Roll in chopped nuts. Serve with crackers.

Bacon Ranch Cheese Ball

16 ounces cream cheese, softened

1 envelope ranch salad dressing mix

1 bunch green onions, diced

8 slices bacon, cooked and crumbled

¼ teaspoon seasoned salt

Combine all ingredients and form into ball. Chill and serve with crackers.

Sweet and Crunchy Cheese Ball

16 ounces cream cheese, softened

1 (4 ounce) package vanilla instant pudding

1 cup powdered sugar

1 (4 ounce) can crushed pineapple, drained

1 cup finely crushed walnuts or pecans

1 cup mini chocolate chips

Mix together first four ingredients. Chill for at least 6 hours or overnight. Form into ball. Stir nuts and chocolate chips together. Roll cheese ball in nut mixture. Serve with regular or chocolate graham cracker sticks.

Baked Brie

½ cup chopped pecans
2½ to 3 tablespoons brown sugar
½ teaspoon cinnamon

1 sheet puff pastry, thawed
1 (8 ounce) Brie wheel, rind intact

Mix together pecans, sugar, and cinnamon. Spread nut mixture onto center of pastry. Place Brie on top of nut mixture. Fold pastry over Brie and pinch pastry closed to seal. Flip pastry over and place on baking sheet lined with parchment paper. Bake at 350 degrees for 20 to 30 minutes until pastry is browned and golden. Serve with crackers.

About the young Redeemer's head,
What wonders and what glories meet!
An unknown star arose and led
The Eastern sages to His feet.

ISAAC WATTS

Stuffed Brie

1 (2 pound) wheel Brie, rind intact
1 carrot, diced
¼ cup chopped sweet onions
2 teaspoons minced garlic
½ cup butter

Pinch saffron
Salt and pepper, to taste
3 tablespoons grated Parmesan cheese
2 sheets puff pastry

Place Brie in freezer for about 20 minutes to firm. Remove from freezer and slice in half horizontally, creating two layers. Sauté vegetables with garlic and butter until tender. Add seasonings and allow to cool. Stir in Parmesan cheese. Place 1 layer of Brie, rind down, on pastry. Spoon on filling and press firmly. Place remaining Brie on top. Roll up pastry to cover Brie and pinch edges to seal. Chill for at least 20 minutes. Bake at 425 degrees for 15 minutes or until golden brown.

Easy Baked Brie

⅛ teaspoon salt

¼ cup toasted almonds, sliced or chopped

¼ cup soft butter

1 (1 pound) wheel Brie

Stir salt into almonds. Spread butter over top of Brie. Sprinkle with almonds. Bake on pan lined with parchment paper at 350 degrees for 10 to 15 minutes until Brie is softened and golden. Serve with crusty bread or crackers.

Holiday Mix

5 cups corn or rice squares cereal

3 cups pretzels of choice

1 teaspoon garlic salt

2 tablespoons Worcestershire sauce

1 (12 ounce) box raisins

1 (20 ounce) container salted peanuts

3 cups red and green candy-coated chocolate pieces

Combine cereal, pretzels, salt, and Worcestershire sauce. Bake in pan for 10 minutes at 300 degrees and allow to cool completely. Combine raisins, peanuts, and candy in separate bowl. Combine peanut mix with cooled cereal mix and serve.

Classic Party Mix

½ cup butter

1¼ teaspoons seasoned salt

4½ teaspoons Worcestershire
sauce

3 cups corn squares cereal

2 cups rice squares cereal

2 cups bran squares cereal

1 cup salted mixed nuts

Heat butter in large roasting pan in oven until melted. Remove. Stir in seasoned salt and Worcestershire sauce. Add cereal and nuts. Mix until all pieces are coated. Bake at 250 degrees for 1 hour, stirring every 15 minutes. Spread on paper towels to cool. Store in airtight container.

Bacon Queso Dip

2 tablespoons chopped onion

1 clove garlic, minced

1 (14.5 ounce) can diced tomatoes, undrained

1 (4 ounce) can diced green chilies, drained

1 teaspoon cumin

½ teaspoon salt

¼ teaspoon pepper

2 pounds processed cheese, cut into pieces

2 slices bacon, cooked and crumbled

Cook onion and garlic in saucepan sprayed with nonstick spray for 2 to 3 minutes. Stir in tomatoes, chilies, cumin, salt, and pepper; blend well. Reduce heat to low and gradually add cheese and bacon, stirring until melted. Serve hot with tortilla chips. Alternately you can put all ingredients in slow cooker and cook on low for 1 to 2 hours. Keep warm to serve.

Pinwheels

8 ounces sour cream

1 (4 ounce) can diced green chilies, drained

1 cup sharp cheddar shredded cheese

1 (4 ounce) can diced black olives, drained

½ cup sweet onion, chopped fine

Garlic salt or seasoned salt, to taste

5 (10 inch) flour tortillas

Mix all filling ingredients together. Spread filling evenly over tortillas. Roll up and cover tightly with plastic wrap. Chill for at least 2 hours. Unwrap and cut into slices. Serve immediately.

Classic Spinach Artichoke Dip

1 (8 ounce) package frozen spinach, thawed and drained

1 (8 ounce) package frozen artichokes, chopped

1 (4 ounce) can diced green chilies, drained

1 cup mayonnaise

⅓ cup grated Parmesan cheese

1 cup shredded mozzarella cheese, divided

2 cloves garlic, minced

Remove excess moisture from spinach in strainer. Combine all ingredients, reserving ¼ cup mozzarella cheese. Bake in preheated 350-degree oven until top is bubbly, about 10 minutes. Top with remaining cheese. Serve with tortilla chips and celery.

Bacon Water Chestnuts

1 pound bacon, each slice cut in half

2 (4 ounce) cans water chestnuts

1½ cups brown sugar

14 ounces ketchup

Pinch garlic powder

Wrap each bacon slice around 1 chestnut and secure with toothpick. Place wrapped water chestnuts on baking sheet under broiler and broil until bacon starts to crisp. Do not burn! Combine brown sugar, ketchup, and garlic powder in 9x13-inch pan. Place wrapped chestnuts in pan and bake at 350 degrees for 10 minutes or until sauce is bubbly. Serve immediately.

Crab Cocktail

12 ounces cream cheese, softened
1 tablespoon lemon juice
1 tablespoon Worcestershire sauce
½ tablespoon diced sweet onion

⅛ teaspoon garlic salt
1 (6 ounce) bottle cocktail sauce
1 (7½ ounce) can crabmeat
2 tablespoons parsley flakes

Cream together first 5 ingredients. Spread mixture in deep pie pan (glass is best). Pour cocktail sauce over mixture. Top with crabmeat. Sprinkle parsley over all. Cover with plastic wrap and refrigerate overnight. Serve chilled with crackers.

Classic Sides and Salads

And there were in the same country shepherds abiding in the field, keeping watch over their flock by night. And, lo, the angel of the Lord came upon them, and the glory of the Lord shone round about them: and they were sore afraid.

Luke 2:8–9

Spiced Cranberries

1½ cups water

4 cups fresh cranberries, washed and stemmed

5 whole cloves

2 tablespoons allspice

3 cinnamon sticks

3 cups sugar

Place water and cranberries in medium saucepan. Tie spices in small cheesecloth bag and add to saucepan. Cover and cook over medium heat just until cranberries burst, about 10 minutes. Remove from heat; discard cheesecloth and spices. Stir in sugar and cook for 5 more minutes on low heat. Cool. Refrigerate for at least 2 hours in covered dish and serve cold.

Gelatin Salad

1 (20 ounce) can crushed pineapple

Water

1 package lemon gelatin

½ cup sugar

¼ teaspoon salt

2 tablespoons lemon juice

1 cup finely grated carrots

1 cup whipping cream

Drain pineapple and reserve juice. Set pineapple aside. Mix pineapple juice with enough water to make 1½ cups of liquid. Heat to boiling. Stir in gelatin until dissolved. Mix in sugar, salt, and lemon juice. Remove from heat and chill until slightly thickened. Add pineapple and carrots. Whip cream until stiff; fold into gelatin mixture. Pour into gelatin mold and chill overnight. Unmold by dipping mold into shallow bowl of hot water and serve.

Red and Green Cucumber Tomato Salad

6 tomatoes, cut into wedges
1 small red onion, sliced
1 cucumber, julienned
1 cup canola oil
½ cup red-wine vinegar
¼ cup chopped fresh parsley

1 clove garlic, minced
½ teaspoon fresh thyme leaves
½ teaspoon fresh marjoram leaves
½ teaspoon fresh basil leaves
1 teaspoon salt
¼ teaspoon freshly ground pepper

Place vegetables in large bowl. Combine remaining ingredients and pour over vegetables. Chill for at least 2 hours.

Italian Pasta Salad

1 cup water

1 large carrot, peeled and chopped

1 cup chopped fresh broccoli

1½ cups rotini, cooked and drained

½ cup zesty Italian salad dressing

1 cup grated Parmesan cheese

Bring water to boil in saucepan. Add carrots and broccoli. Boil for 3 to 5 minutes until carrots begin to get tender. Drain and combine with remaining ingredients. Mix well.

Festive Cranberry Salad

8 ounces cream cheese, softened

2 tablespoons mayonnaise

2 tablespoons sugar

1 (16 ounce) can whole cranberry sauce

1 (9 ounce) can crushed pineapple, drained

2 cups whipped topping

Combine cream cheese, mayonnaise, and sugar. Add cranberries and pineapple. Stir. Fold in whipped cream. Pour into oblong or square container. Cover and freeze for up to 2 months. To serve, allow to sit at room temperature for 30 minutes. Cut into squares.

Old-Fashioned Pork and Beans

2 large sweet onions, chopped

2 garlic cloves, minced

½ pound sliced bacon, cooked and diced

4 (16 ounce) cans pork and beans

½ pound cooked ham, chunked

1½ cups brown sugar

1 teaspoon parsley

2 medium lemons, juiced

½ cup barbecue sauce

1 teaspoon salt

⅛ teaspoon pepper

Cook onion and garlic in skillet used to cook bacon. Remove from heat. Add pork and beans, ham chunks, brown sugar, parsley, lemon juice, barbecue sauce, reserved cooked bacon, salt, and pepper. Mix well and pour into deep baking dish. Cover and bake at 350 degrees for 40 minutes or until bubbly.

Coleslaw

1 medium head cabbage, shredded
1 teaspoon salt
3 large carrots, grated
1 small sweet onion, sliced thin
2 cups sugar

¼ cup water
1 cup apple cider vinegar
1 teaspoon celery seed
½ teaspoon mustard seed

Combine cabbage, salt, carrots, and onion. Toss and refrigerate for 1 hour. Meanwhile, bring sugar, water, and vinegar to a boil. Remove from heat and stir in celery seed and mustard seed. Cool completely. Pour over cabbage and cover. Chill for at least 2 hours. Serve cold.

Make-Ahead Creamed Corn

18 cups corn cut off the cob

1 pound butter

1 pint half-and-half

1 tablespoon freezer salt

1 tablespoon sugar

Mix all ingredients together in large roasting pan. Bake uncovered for 1 hour at 325 degrees. Stir every 15 minutes. It's normal for corn to look slightly curdled. Allow to cool. Package in freezer bags or containers. Freeze for up to 6 months. To serve, remove desired amount and thaw in refrigerator or microwave. Heat until warm.

Somehow, not only at Christmas
But all the long year through,
The joy that you give to others
Is the joy that comes back to you.

JOHN GREENLEAF WHITTIER

Southern Chicken Gravy

3 tablespoons fried chicken drippings

3 tablespoons flour

2½ cups milk

½ cup heavy cream

Salt and pepper, to taste

Leave 3 tablespoons of drippings in skillet. Stir in flour until well blended; cook over medium heat for 2 to 3 minutes or until bubbly. Gradually add milk and cream. Boil until thick and smooth, stirring constantly. Add salt and pepper to taste.

Simple Turkey Gravy

Turkey pan drippings

¼ cup flour

Water

Salt and pepper, to taste

Pour turkey pan drippings into 2-cup measuring cup and skim off ¼ cup of fat; set aside. Add enough water to drippings to make 2 cups of liquid. Place reserved ¼ cup fat into saucepan and stir in flour. Pour the 2 cups of liquid into flour mixture. Cook, stirring until thickened and bubbly. Add salt and pepper to taste.

Southern Giblet Gravy

Giblets from 1 turkey
4 cups cold water
4 tablespoons butter
4 tablespoons flour
2 cups turkey pan drippings

½ cup half-and-half
½ teaspoon salt
½ teaspoon pepper
2 hard-boiled eggs, chopped

Remove liver from giblets and refrigerate. Place giblets in saucepan; cover with water and bring to a boil. Reduce heat and simmer for about 1 hour. Add liver and simmer for another 30 minutes. Drain in colander and allow to cool. Chop giblets and set aside. Melt butter in heavy saucepan and stir in flour. Cook and stir for about 3 minutes. Slowly stir in drippings and half-and-half. Continue cooking and stirring until thickened. Add salt and pepper. Stir in eggs and giblets. Serve warm.

Ranch Macaroni Salad

3 cups macaroni, uncooked
2 cups frozen baby peas
2 cups diced cooked ham

2 cups shredded cheddar cheese
1 cup ranch dressing
1 tablespoon bacon pieces

Cook pasta according to package directions. Place peas in strainer and drain cooked pasta over peas to thaw. Combine all ingredients in large bowl. Chill for 2 hours before serving.

Candied Carrots

6 large carrots, peeled
12 small white onions, peeled
3 tablespoons butter
1 tablespoon sugar

⅓ cup light molasses
¼ teaspoon salt
¼ teaspoon ginger
¼ teaspoon allspice

In separate medium saucepans, cook carrots and onions, covered, in boiling salted water for 20 minutes or just until tender. Drain and set aside. Melt butter in large skillet; stir in sugar, molasses, salt, and spices. Heat to boiling, stirring constantly. Add carrots and onions, stirring to coat well with syrup. Simmer, stirring frequently, for about 10 minutes.

Gingered Sweet Potatoes

6 large sweet potatoes

1 cup firmly packed light brown sugar, divided

½ cup butter, melted

⅓ cup half-and-half

2 large eggs

1 teaspoon vanilla

2 tablespoons flour

¼ cup cold butter, cut into pieces

2 cups gingersnap cookies, crumbled

Cook sweet potatoes in boiling water to cover over medium heat for 30 minutes or until tender. Cool; peel and mash potatoes. In mixing bowl, combine mashed sweet potatoes, ½ cup brown sugar, melted butter, half-and-half, eggs, and vanilla. Beat at medium speed until smooth. Spoon into greased 9x13-inch baking dish. Combine ½ cup brown sugar and flour. Cut in ¼ cup cold butter with pastry blender until crumbly. Stir in crumbled gingersnaps. Sprinkle mixture over sweet potatoes. Bake uncovered at 350 degrees for 25 minutes or until topping is lightly browned.

Garlic Ranch Mashed Potatoes

2 pounds potatoes peeled and diced

¾ cup hot milk

6 tablespoons butter

1 tablespoon garlic salt

2 tablespoons ranch dressing

Boil potatoes until soft. Mash with remaining ingredients.

Strawberry Salad

2 (8 ounce) packages cream cheese, softened

2 tablespoons mayonnaise

2 tablespoons sugar

2 (10 ounce) packages frozen strawberries, partially thawed and sweetened

2 cups mini marshmallows

1 (12 ounce) can crushed pineapple, drained

3½ cups whipped topping

½ cup chopped walnuts

In large bowl, blend cream cheese, mayonnaise, and sugar. Add remaining ingredients. Pour into festive gelatin mold and put in freezer. Freeze thoroughly. Take salad out 15 to 20 minutes before serving. Cut and serve.

Cheesy Mashed Potatoes

3 pounds potatoes, peeled and quartered

1½ sticks butter

6 ounces cream cheese, softened

1 cup shredded cheddar cheese, divided

1 small green pepper, finely chopped

6 green onions, finely chopped

½ cup grated Parmesan cheese

¼ cup milk

1 teaspoon salt

Cook potatoes in enough boiling water to cover for 15 minutes or until tender; drain and mash. Add butter and cream cheese; beat at medium speed with electric mixer until smooth. Stir in ½ cup cheddar cheese, green pepper, onions, Parmesan cheese, milk, and salt. Spoon into lightly buttered 7x11-inch baking dish. Bake at 350 degrees for 30 to 40 minutes or until thoroughly heated. Sprinkle with remaining cheese; bake for 5 minutes or until cheese melts.

Bread Stuffing

½ cup butter

1 cup chopped sweet onion

½ cup chopped celery, with leaves

8 cups bread cubes

2 tablespoons hot chicken or turkey broth

1 teaspoon salt

¼ teaspoon pepper

1 teaspoon sage

½ teaspoon thyme

½ teaspoon marjoram

For a soft, moist dressing, use fresh or slightly stale bread. For a lighter, fluffier dressing, use dried stale (but not moldy!) bread.

Melt butter in frying pan. Add onion and celery, and cook until soft but not browned. Combine butter mixture with bread cubes, broth, and seasonings. Stuff turkey; roast. Makes enough for an 8-to-10-pound turkey.

Green Bean Casserole

1 pound French-style frozen green beans

1 small onion, halved and thinly sliced

1 teaspoon parsley

3 tablespoons butter, divided

2 tablespoons flour

½ teaspoon lemon zest

½ teaspoon salt

Dash pepper

½ cup milk

1 cup sour cream

½ cup shredded mild cheddar cheese

¼ cup dry bread crumbs

Cook frozen beans according to package directions; drain. Cook onion and parsley in 2 tablespoons butter until onion is tender. Stir in flour, lemon zest, salt, and pepper. Add milk and cook until thickened and bubbly, stirring constantly. Add sour cream to green beans and stir in hot milk mixture. Heat until sauce begins to bubble. Spoon into 1½-quart casserole. Sprinkle cheese over top. Melt remaining 1 tablespoon butter and toss with bread crumbs. Sprinkle over cheese. Broil for 1 to 2 minutes about 5 inches from broiler until cheese melts and crumbs brown.

Broccoli Rice Casserole

1 cup chopped onion

2 tablespoons butter

1 (10 ounce) can cream of chicken
    or mushroom soup

1 teaspoon salt

½ teaspoon ground black pepper

3 cups cooked rice

1 (10 ounce) package frozen
    chopped broccoli, thawed

2 cups shredded cheddar cheese

In large skillet, cook onion in butter until tender-crisp. Add soup, salt, and pepper. Mix well. Spoon into buttered 2-quart baking dish. Bake at 350 degrees for 35 minutes or until hot and bubbly.

To add a Christmas ambience to any party, compile a CD or playlist of holiday instrumental music. Having Christmas carols play in the background is nice, but instrumental music is best so that friends and family can have uninterrupted conversation without the distraction of other voices.

Creamed Onions

2 pounds small white and red onions, peeled

½ teaspoon salt

2 tablespoons butter

2 tablespoons flour

1½ cups whole milk

¼ teaspoon Cajun seasoning

¼ teaspoon paprika

Salt and pepper, to taste

Place onions in medium saucepan. Add ½ teaspoon salt and enough water to cover. Bring onions to a boil. Cover and cook for 20 minutes or until tender. Drain and reserve cooking liquid. Set onions and cooking liquid aside. In same saucepan, melt butter and stir in flour. Gradually add milk. Cook, stirring constantly, until mixture thickens and begins to bubble. Stir in Cajun seasoning and paprika. Add salt and pepper. Add some of reserved liquid to thin sauce, if needed. Add onions to sauce and heat through.

Zucchini Casserole

2 large zucchini, cut in ¼-inch slices

2 celery stalks, chopped

1 medium onion, chopped

1 medium green pepper, chopped

1 cup fresh mushrooms, sliced

1 cup old-fashioned rolled oats

1 (16 ounce) can tomato sauce

2 teaspoons oregano

¼ teaspoon dried basil

½ teaspoon marjoram

½ teaspoon rosemary leaves

1 teaspoon dried red pepper

2 cloves garlic, crushed

Salt and pepper, to taste

½ cup grated Parmesan cheese

Prepare vegetables and layer in order listed in medium casserole dish. Sprinkle with rolled oats. Set aside. In medium bowl, mix tomato sauce and seasonings. Stir well and pour sauce over vegetable mixture. Sprinkle Parmesan cheese over casserole. Bake uncovered at 350 degrees for 45 minutes or until vegetables are tender.

Scalloped Corn

1 cup half-and-half

3 large eggs

1 tablespoon sugar

¼ teaspoon salt

⅛ teaspoon pepper

¼ cup finely chopped sweet onion

2 cups frozen cream-style corn, thawed

1 cup coarsely crushed cracker crumbs

In large bowl, whisk half-and-half and eggs together. Add remaining ingredients and mix well. Pour into lightly buttered casserole dish. Bake at 350 degrees for 40 minutes or until almost set. Let stand for 5 minutes before serving.

Sweet Potato Casserole

2 large sweet potatoes
3 eggs, beaten
¼ cup melted butter
⅔ cup evaporated milk

Topping:
1 cup chopped pecans
½ cup brown sugar
¼ cup flour
2 tablespoons butter, melted

Wash, peel, and cut up sweet potatoes. Boil for about 25 minutes, until tender. Drain well and mash. Stir in eggs, butter, and evaporated milk. Spoon into greased baking dish. Combine topping ingredients and sprinkle evenly over sweet potatoes. Bake at 350 degrees for 40 minutes or until set.

Salmon Cakes

½ cup dry bread crumbs

1 stalk celery, very finely chopped

2 tablespoons mayonnaise

2 tablespoons finely chopped onion

1 tablespoon parsley flakes

1 teaspoon lemon pepper seasoning

1 teaspoon baking powder

1 egg, beaten

1 (16 ounce) can pink salmon, drained and deboned

Place all ingredients except salmon in large bowl and mix well. Add salmon and mix gently but thoroughly. Shape into 4 patties. Place patties on lightly greased broiler pan and broil for 4 minutes on each side about 8 inches from source of heat.

Seven-Layer Salad

6 cups chopped lettuce

Salt and pepper, to taste

6 hard-boiled eggs, sliced

2 cups frozen peas, thawed

1½ cups bacon, crisply cooked and crumbled

2 cups shredded cheddar cheese

1 cup mayonnaise

2 tablespoons sugar

¼ cup sliced green onion

Dash paprika

Place 3 cups of lettuce in bottom of large bowl and sprinkle with salt and pepper. Layer egg slices over lettuce in bowl and sprinkle with more salt and pepper. Continue to layer vegetables in this order: peas, remaining lettuce, crumbled bacon, and shredded cheese, along with light sprinklings of salt and pepper. Combine mayonnaise and sugar and blend well. Spread over top to edge of bowl, covering entire salad. Cover and refrigerate overnight. Toss before serving. Garnish with green onion and paprika.

Classic Mashed Potatoes

8 medium potatoes, peeled and sliced

½ to ⅔ cup whole milk

⅓ cup butter

1 teaspoon salt

¼ teaspoon sugar

Dash pepper

Cook potatoes until tender in enough boiling water to cover. Drain and mash. Add ½ cup milk and remaining ingredients. Add more milk, if needed, for desired consistency. Serve hot.

Ambrosia Salad

1 cup fruit cocktail, drained
½ cup mandarin oranges
½ cup pineapple tidbits
¼ cup maraschino cherries, halved

¼ cup red seedless grapes
½ cup mini marshmallows
½ cup sour cream
Lettuce leaves

Drain all of the fruits. Combine all ingredients except lettuce in large bowl. Mix gently but thoroughly. Chill. Serve on lettuce leaves and garnish with additional festive fruits.

Corn Bread Dressing

3½ cups crumbled corn bread
3½ cups crumbled biscuits
½ cup melted butter
½ cup minced onion
1 cup chopped celery

½ teaspoon pepper
2 eggs, slightly beaten
3 cups chicken or turkey broth
Savory seasoning, to taste
Salt, to taste

Place crumbled corn bread and crumbled biscuits in roasting pan. Add remaining ingredients. Mix together gently with hands. Place in greased shallow baking pan. Bake uncovered at 400 degrees for 15 to 25 minutes.

Baked Beans

1 pound dry navy beans
6 cups cold water
1 teaspoon salt
12 slices bacon

½ cup brown sugar
¼ cup molasses
1 medium onion, chopped
2 teaspoons dry mustard

Rinse beans. Combine beans and water in large saucepan or Dutch oven. Cover; bring to a boil. Boil for 2 minutes. Remove from heat; let stand for 1 hour or overnight. Add salt. Simmer partially covered for 1 hour or until beans are tender. Drain, reserving liquid. Cut bacon into 1-inch pieces. Combine uncooked bacon, brown sugar, molasses, onion, and dry mustard with beans in Dutch oven or 2-quart bean pot. Add 1¾ cups reserved liquid. Bake uncovered at 300 degrees for 5 hours. Add additional water if necessary.

Stuffed Squash

3 small butternut squash
1 large sweet onion, diced
1 tablespoon olive oil
1 cup finely diced celery
1 cup fresh spinach, coarsely chopped

1 cup whole wheat bread crumbs
¼ teaspoon salt
¼ cup finely ground almonds
2 tablespoons butter

Clean squash and cut each in half. Bake at 350 degrees for 35 minutes or until tender. Sauté onions in oil until soft. Add diced celery. Cover and simmer on medium heat until tender. Add spinach; stir to wilt. Combine bread crumbs with salt and ground nuts. Stuff squashes with spinach and sprinkle crumb mixture on top. Dot with butter. Return to oven for 10 to 15 minutes.

Winter Squash Casserole

4 medium yellow squash, sliced

½ cup chopped onion

¼ cup melted butter

2 hard-cooked eggs, chopped

½ cup shredded cheddar cheese

½ cup butter cracker crumbs

Cook sliced squash in small amount of boiling salted water for 10 minutes or until tender. Drain and set aside. Sauté onion in butter until tender. Combine drained squash, sautéed onion, butter, chopped eggs, and cheddar cheese in 1-quart casserole dish. Top with buttercracker crumbs. Bake at 350 degrees for 20 minutes.

Apple-Cranberry Casserole

4 cups chopped peeled apples

2 cups fresh cranberries

¾ cup sugar

1 stick butter

½ cup brown sugar

⅓ cup flour

1 cup old-fashioned oats, uncooked

½ cup chopped pecans or walnuts

Place apples and cranberries in greased 9x13-inch casserole dish. Sprinkle with sugar. Do not mix. Melt butter in medium saucepan over low heat. Add brown sugar, flour, oats, and nuts. Pour over apples and cranberries. Bake at 350 degrees for about 1 hour. Serve with your holiday turkey.

Spinach Bake

2 (10 ounce) packages frozen
   spinach

6 ounces cream cheese, softened

½ cup butter, melted, divided

1 cup Italian bread crumbs

Dash paprika

Thaw spinach and press to remove excess water. Lightly butter
casserole dish and set aside. In large mixing bowl, combine spinach,
cream cheese, and ¼ cup melted butter. Spoon into prepared dish.
Sprinkle with bread crumbs and paprika. Top with remaining ¼ cup
butter. Bake at 350 degrees for 25 minutes.

Sausage Cashew Casserole

1 pound pork sausage
½ cup chopped onion
¼ cup chopped green pepper
¼ cup chopped celery
1 cup rice, uncooked

1 (14 ounce) can cream of chicken soup
1 (14 ounce) can chicken broth
1 small can mushrooms, with juice
¼ cup chopped cashews

Brown sausage. Remove sausage from pan and sauté onion, green pepper, and celery in drippings. Remove from heat. Add sausage and remaining ingredients. Spoon into casserole dish. Bake at 350 degrees for about 1 hour.

You can never truly enjoy Christmas until you can look up into the Father's face and tell Him you have received His Christmas gift.

JOHN R. RICE

Leah's Sausage Stuffing

1½ cups diced celery

¾ cup diced onion

1 tablespoon plus ¾ cup melted butter, divided

1 pound sage-flavored breakfast sausage

8 cups bread cubes

¼ teaspoon pepper

1 teaspoon thyme

1 tablespoon parsley flakes

1 (14 ounce) can chicken broth

2 pears, peeled and diced

2 apples, peeled and diced (Granny Smith or Macintosh)

½ cup dried cranberries

Preheat oven to 350 degrees. Sauté celery and onion in 1 tablespoon butter until tender; remove from pan and put in large mixing bowl. Brown sausage then add to mixing bowl. Add remaining ingredients; mix to coat. Place in large baking dish and bake covered for 25 minutes. Remove cover and bake for 15 minutes or until browned.

Traditional Main Courses and Brunches

And the angel said unto them, Fear not: for, behold, I bring you good tidings of great joy, which shall be to all people. For unto you is born this day in the city of David a Saviour, which is Christ the Lord.

LUKE 2:10–11

Traditional Stuffed Turkey

1 (14 to 16 pound) turkey
1 cup fresh mushrooms, chopped
2 cups cooked chopped celery
1 cup chopped onion
½ cup butter

½ teaspoon dried savory leaves, crushed
1 (14 ounce) package herb-seasoned cubed stuffing
1 cup cooked wild rice
1¾ cups chicken or turkey broth

Wash turkey under cold running water. Remove neck and giblets from inside turkey and save for making giblet gravy. In large saucepan over medium heat, sauté mushrooms, celery, and onion in butter with savory leaves until tender. Remove from heat. Add stuffing, rice, and broth. Mix well. Spoon stuffing mixture into neck and body cavities lightly; do not compress. Sew opening closed with butcher's string. Tie legs together. Place turkey, breast side up, on a rack in deep roasting pan. Roast uncovered at 325 degrees for 4 hours or until internal temperature reaches 180 degrees. Baste turkey occasionally with pan drippings and butter. When skin turns golden, cover loosely with tent of aluminum foil until done.

Christmas Ham

1 (12 to 16 pound) Virginia ham

2 cups unsulphured molasses, divided

1 cup cider vinegar

3 cloves garlic

3 bay leaves

1 teaspoon peppercorns

Whole cloves

½ pound dark brown sugar

Juice from large jar of sweet pickles

Begin preparing ham two days before serving. In large stockpot, cover ham with cold water. Add 1 cup molasses and cider vinegar. Allow to stand in cool place overnight. The next day, remove ham and pour off liquid. Cover ham with fresh cold water and add remaining 1 cup molasses, garlic cloves, bay leaves, peppercorns, and a few whole cloves. Bring to rolling boil over high heat and cover. Reduce heat slightly and boil for another 30 minutes. Turn off heat but do not remove cover. Let stand in cool place overnight. Remove ham from water. Remove any rind. Using sharp knife, score ham diagonally. Push in whole cloves in an even pattern to decorate and add flavor. Put ham in roaster, fattest side up. Mix brown sugar with pickle juice, adding just enough juice until a paste is formed. Spread ham with brown sugar paste. Bake at 350 degrees for about 60 minutes or until ham is nicely glazed.

Roast Turkey

1 (16 to 18 pound) turkey

Kosher salt

1 tablespoon dried rosemary, crumbled

2 teaspoons ground sage

2 teaspoons dried thyme, crumbled

1½ teaspoons salt

1 teaspoon pepper

1 stick butter, melted

Garlic powder

Paprika

1 (14 ounce) can broth, for basting

Choose a plump turkey. Clean and dry thoroughly inside and out. Remove neck and giblets from inside turkey and rub liberally with kosher salt. Combine rosemary, sage, thyme, salt, and pepper in small bowl. Rub some in each cavity. If adding stuffing, pack body cavity loosely with stuffing. If turkey is being stuffed, sew opening closed. Tuck in wings and fold tail in over stuffing. Brush top of turkey generously with melted butter, and sprinkle with garlic powder, paprika, salt and pepper. Roast turkey uncovered at 375 degrees, basting frequently with melted butter and broth, or with pan juices.

After 1 hour, baste and sprinkle with seasonings again, then make tent with aluminum foil and cover breast loosely. Reduce heat to 325 degrees and continue roasting for 1 hour, basting occasionally. Uncover breast and continue roasting for 2 hours longer or until a thermometer inserted in thickest portion of thigh registers 165 degrees. When turkey is golden brown and done, allow to rest for 20 minutes before carving. Transfer turkey to serving platter. Reserve pan drippings for gravy.

Festive Ham and Pineapples

1 (7 pound) smoked ham

2 cups water

Whole cloves

1 cup brown sugar

2 tablespoons flour

⅛ teaspoon garlic powder

⅛ teaspoon onion powder

⅛ teaspoon black pepper

1 (16 ounce) can sliced pineapple rings

1 jar maraschino cherries, cut into halves

Olive oil spray

Place ham in roaster with water. Cover and bake at 325 degrees for 3½ to 4½ hours. If ham has an exposed bone, cover it with foil. Keep an eye on ham as it cooks and spray occasionally with olive oil during first part of cooking. Continue roasting until thermometer inserted in center reads 160 degrees. Be sure thermometer is not touching bone. When ham is done, remove from oven. Lift off rind. Using sharp knife, score fat surface crosswise and dot with cloves. Set aside. Combine brown sugar and flour. Rub mixture over scored ham. Sprinkle lightly with garlic powder, onion powder, and black pepper. Place a pineapple slice ham so one of the cloves will be in the center of the circle. Cover clove with maraschino cherry half. Each cherry half should be placed in the center of a pineapple slice. Continue until ham is covered decoratively with pineapple slices and cherries. Brown, uncovered, at 400 degrees for 20 minutes.

Holiday Ham Steaks

4 to 6 ham slices, about ½ inch thick

1¼ cups cranberry juice

½ cup light brown sugar

½ cup raisins

½ cup orange juice

2 tablespoons cornstarch

Dash ground cloves

Arrange ham steaks evenly in 9x13-inch inch baking dish. In saucepan, combine remaining ingredients. Cook and stir over medium heat until thick and bubbly. Pour over ham steaks. Bake uncovered at 350 degrees for 30 to 40 minutes. Great for Christmas morning!

Stuffed Cornish Hen

1 (6 ounce) package wild rice mix
½ cup diced celery
1 (5 ounce) can water chestnuts, sliced
½ cup chopped mushrooms
¼ cup butter, melted
1 tablespoon soy sauce
4 (1 pound) Cornish game hens

Cook rice according to package directions; cool. Add celery, water chestnuts, mushrooms, butter, and soy sauce. Toss lightly to mix. Salt inside of birds, stuff with mixture, and truss. Cook at 450 degrees for 15 minutes, reduce heat to 375 degrees, and cook for 30 minutes longer or until juices run clear.

Herb-Roasted Turkey with Maple Glaze

1 (12 to 14 pound) turkey
Salt and pepper
1 orange, unpeeled
1 Granny Smith apple, unpeeled
1 medium sweet onion
5 tablespoons butter, softened

2 teaspoons thyme
½ teaspoon dried rosemary
½ teaspoon marjoram
⅓ cup maple syrup
¼ cup brown sugar
¼ cup apple cider

Clean turkey inside and out. Sprinkle cavity with salt and pepper. Place turkey on rack in open roasting pan, breast side up. Cut orange, apple, and onion into large chunks and stuff into turkey cavity. Tie legs together with twine. Sprinkle all over with salt and pepper. Combine butter with dried herbs in small bowl. Separate skin from breasts and push most of butter mixture evenly under each side. Rub turkey all over with any remaining butter mixture. Wrap wing tips and drumstick ends with small pieces of foil. Loosely tent turkey with large piece of foil. Roast at 325 degrees for 2½ hours. Remove and discard foil tent. Combine maple syrup, brown sugar, and apple cider. Baste with maple mixture. Continue roasting, basting frequently, for 1 hour longer, or until meat thermometer registers about 180 degrees when inserted in thickest part of turkey thigh.

Shrimp and Scallop Casserole

½ cup chopped green pepper

1 cup chopped celery

½ cup chopped onion

2 tablespoons butter

2 pounds fresh cooked shrimp

1 pound fresh cooked scallops

1 cup cooked rice

1 small jar pimentos, drained and chopped

¾ cup half-and-half

1 (10 ounce) can cream of mushroom soup

1 cup mayonnaise

1 tablespoon Worcestershire sauce

Dash white pepper

Sauté green pepper, celery, and onion in butter. Toss all ingredients together and put in buttered baking dish. Bake uncovered at 375 degrees for 35 minutes or until heated through.

Beef and Broccoli with Mushrooms

1 tablespoon butter
¾ pound thin beef strips
1 small sweet onion, sliced
2 cups fresh broccoli florets

½ cup fresh mushrooms, sliced
1 (2 ounce) package brown gravy mix
1 cup water
¼ teaspoon pepper

In large skillet, heat butter over medium-high heat. Add beef strips and onion and sauté for 3 to 4 minutes; add broccoli and mushrooms. In separate bowl, combine gravy mix, water, and pepper. Pour over beef mixture. Stir and bring to a boil. Cover and simmer for 5 to 8 minutes or until broccoli is tender.

Herb-Roasted Chicken Breast

¼ cup flour

½ teaspoon salt

⅛ teaspoon pepper

6 boneless, skinless chicken breasts

3 tablespoons olive oil

2 cloves garlic

1 large onion, chopped

¼ teaspoon thyme

¼ teaspoon oregano

¼ teaspoon rosemary

2 teaspoons fresh parsley, minced

½ cup chicken broth

Measure flour, salt, and pepper into resealable plastic bag. Shake chicken in bag until well coated. In heavy skillet, combine olive oil, garlic, and onion. Cook for 2 to 3 minutes on medium heat. Add coated chicken and brown evenly on both sides until golden but not cooked through. Transfer to casserole dish. Combine remaining ingredients and baste chicken. Continue to baste during cooking. Bake at 375 degrees for 50 minutes or until tender and juices run clear. Serve with vegetables and rice.

Veal Parmesan

6 frozen veal cube steaks
Salt and pepper, to taste
2 tablespoons olive oil
1 (8 ounce) can tomato sauce
½ cup vegetable broth

1 (4 ounce) can sliced mushrooms, drained
2 tablespoons grated Parmesan cheese
½ teaspoon oregano
6 slices mozzarella cheese

Season steaks with salt and pepper and brown in hot oil. Add tomato sauce and broth. Add mushrooms, Parmesan cheese, and oregano. Cover and simmer for 10 to 15 minutes or until steaks are cooked through. Place slice of mozzarella cheese on each steak, spooning sauce over cheese until cheese is melted. Serve over cooked spaghetti.

It is good to be children sometimes, and never better than at Christmas, when its mighty founder was a child himself.

CHARLES DICKENS

Parrish Christmas Brunch Casserole

2 (8 count) tubes refrigerated crescent rolls
2 tablespoons butter
1 small onion, chopped
1 green pepper, chopped
½ cup chopped mushrooms
8 eggs
1 package sausage links
2 cups shredded cheddar cheese

Preheat oven according to crescent roll package directions. Press crescent rolls into 9x12-inch pan, pressing halfway up sides. Melt butter in saucepan. Sauté onions, green peppers, and mushrooms in butter. Set aside. In same saucepan, scramble eggs. Meanwhile, in separate saucepan, brown sausage links. Cool. Cut into small pieces. Layer eggs, onions, peppers, mushrooms, sausage, and cheese on top of crescent roll crust. Bake as directed on crescent roll package or until done.

Cheesy Hash Brown Bake

1 pound frozen hash browns, prepared according to package

10 eggs, scrambled with butter, salt, and pepper to taste

1 pound breakfast sausage, browned and drained

2 cups shredded sharp cheddar cheese

In buttered 9x13-inch baking pan, layer hash browns, scrambled eggs, sausage, and cheese. Bake at 350 degrees until cheese is melted and center is heated, about 25 minutes.

Breakfast Pizza

1 (8 count) tube refrigerated crescent rolls

1 pound bulk sausage, cooked and drained

1 cup frozen hash browns, thawed

1 cup shredded sharp cheddar cheese

5 eggs

¼ cup milk

½ teaspoon salt

¼ teaspoon pepper

Press rolls in slightly greased 12-inch pizza pan. Seal perforations. Spoon sausage over crust. Sprinkle with potatoes. Top with cheddar cheese. In bowl, beat together remaining ingredients. Pour onto crust. Bake at 375 degrees for 25 minutes.

Slow Cooker Brunch

4 cups sliced and buttered french bread, cubed

1 (16 ounce) package frozen spinach

6 to 8 slices bacon diced and cooked

2 cups shredded cheddar cheese

1 (10 ounce) can cream of mushroom soup

½ cup evaporated milk

5 eggs

1 teaspoon salt

¼ teaspoon pepper

1 tablespoon minced dried onion

Lightly butter slow cooker. Layer with half of buttered bread cubes, spinach, bacon, and cheese. Repeat layers, ending with cheese. Whisk together remaining ingredients. Pour over slow cooker mixture. Chill for at least 1 hour. Cook on low for 4 hours.

Prepare a Christmas brunch casserole on Christmas Eve so that it's ready to go in the oven first thing in the morning—after stockings are opened and before the presents! Plan for one of your meals to be a slow cooker meal (recipes follow) to make your holiday prep even simpler.

Gingersnap Brisket Dinner

2 (2 ounce) packages onion soup mix

4 pounds beef brisket

1 teaspoon salt

¼ teaspoon pepper

1 teaspoon garlic salt

2 cups water

6 gingersnap cookies, crumbled

1 (12 ounce) bottle chili sauce

1 large sweet onion, sliced

2 cups baby carrots

4 to 6 small red potatoes

Put onion soup mix into slow cooker. Season brisket with salt, pepper, and garlic salt. Add brisket to slow cooker. Cover with water and add gingersnaps. Cover top of brisket with chili sauce. Add vegetables and cook on low for 6 to 8 hours or until meat and vegetables are tender.

Slow Cooker Mango Ham

3 pounds fully cooked boneless
   ham
¼ teaspoon pepper

2 (6 ounce) jars mango chutney
1 onion, chopped fine
1 tablespoon apple cider vinegar

Place ham in slow cooker. Mix remaining ingredients in medium bowl and pour over ham. Cook on low for 6 to 8 hours or until thoroughly heated. Slice and serve in sandwiches or with mashed potatoes.

Slow Cooker Cranberry Pork Roast

1 (2 to 3 pound) boneless pork shoulder roast, trimmed

2 cups baby carrots

2 cups quartered potatoes

1 cup sweetened dried cranberries

1 cup chicken broth

½ cup cranberry juice cocktail

½ teaspoon salt

⅛ teaspoon pepper

Place roast and vegetables in slow cooker. Combine cranberries, broth, cranberry juice cocktail, and salt and pepper in small bowl. Pour over roast. Cover and cook on low for 7 to 9 hours.

Swiss Chicken

6 boneless, skinless chicken
   breasts

6 slices baby Swiss cheese

1 (10 ounce) can cream of
   mushroom soup

⅛ teaspoon pepper

¼ cup milk

2 cups stuffing mix

½ cup margarine, melted

Lightly grease slow cooker. Place chicken breasts in slow cooker and top with cheese. Combine soup, pepper, and milk, stirring well. Spoon soup mixture over cheese and sprinkle with stuffing mix. Drizzle margarine over stuffing mix. Cook on high for 4 to 6 hours or until done.

Citrus Pork Chops

3 cloves garlic, minced
2 teaspoons salt
1 teaspoon pepper
1 tablespoon soy sauce

1 tablespoon lemon juice
2 tablespoons orange juice
4 medium pork chops
¼ cup flour

Mix all ingredients except pork chops and flour. Dip chops into mixture and then coat with flour. Lightly brown chops in large skillet and then place in slow cooker. Cook on low for 10 hours.

Slow Cooker Barbecue Pork Roast

1 (3 pound) boneless pork roast
½ cup chopped onion
4 small red potatoes
1 (16 ounce) bag baby carrots

½ cup barbecue sauce
¼ cup honey
½ teaspoon salt
¼ teaspoon pepper

Place pork, onions, potatoes, and carrots in slow-cooker. Combine barbecue sauce, honey, salt, and pepper in small bowl and pour into slow cooker. Cover and cook on low for 8 to 10 hours or until meat is tender.

Slow Cooker Chicken Divan

1 pound boneless, skinless chicken breasts

½ small onion, chopped

1 (10 ounce) can cream of chicken soup

⅓ cup mayonnaise

3 tablespoons flour

2 stalks celery, diced

2 cups baby carrots

½ teaspoon curry powder

1 tablespoon lemon juice

1 (10 ounce) package frozen broccoli cuts

Lightly grease slow cooker. Add all ingredients except broccoli. Mix well. Cover and cook on low for 8 to 10 hours or until chicken is done. Add broccoli during last hour of cooking. Serve alone or over hot buttered noodles.

Slow Cooker Cranberry Chicken

2 pounds boneless, skinless
chicken breasts

1 (8 ounce) bottle French salad
dressing

1 (2 ounce package) onion soup
mix

1 (10 ounce) can whole cranberry
sauce

Add all ingredients to slow cooker and stir to coat chicken. Cook on
low for 8 hours. Serve over rice or pasta.

Slow Cooker Meatloaf Dinner

½ cup milk

1½ cups Italian bread crumbs

2 pounds ground beef

2 eggs

1 small onion, chopped

1½ teaspoons salt

½ teaspoon pepper

1 teaspoon yellow mustard

1 (12 ounce) can whole tomatoes

2 to 4 medium baking potatoes, pricked with fork

Mix all ingredients well, except tomatoes and potatoes. Shape into loaf and place in slow cooker. Top with potatoes. Drain tomatoes and pour into slow cooker. Cover and cook on low for 5 to 7 hours or until done.

Take Christ out of Christmas,
and December becomes the bleakest
and most colorless month of the year.

A. F. WELLS

Corned Beef and Sauerkraut

1 tablespoon Dijon mustard
4 slices rye bread
1 (12 ounce) can corned beef
1 pound sauerkraut, drained

1 (10 ounce) can tomato soup
¼ cup water
4 slices Swiss cheese

Spread mustard on each slice of bread and cut into small squares.
Scatter over bottom of greased microwaveable dish. Crumble corned
beef and spread on top of bread. Mix sauerkraut, soup, and water.
Pour over corned beef. Cover with wax paper. Microwave on high for
8 minutes, turning twice during cooking. Add cheese and microwave
uncovered on high for 1 more minute. Let stand for 5 minutes before
serving. Season to taste and top with relish if desired.

New Year's Casserole

2 pounds sausage
1 can sauerkraut

1 large sweet onion, cut into rings
5 potatoes, sliced thin

In baking dish, layer sausage, then sauerkraut, onion rings, and potatoes. Cover and bake at 375 degrees for 1½ hours or until potatoes are done. Uncover and brown for the last 15 minutes.

Breads and Sweets

And this shall be a sign unto you; Ye shall find the babe wrapped in swaddling clothes, lying in a manger. And suddenly there was with the angel a multitude of the heavenly host praising God, and saying, Glory to God in the highest, and on earth peace, good will toward men.

LUKE 2:12–14

Gingerbread

2¼ cups flour
1 cup dark molasses
½ cup shortening
1 teaspoon soda
1¼ teaspoons cinnamon

⅓ cup sugar
¾ cup hot water
1 egg
1 teaspoon ginger
¾ teaspoon salt

Mix all ingredients in large mixing bowl. Pour into greased 9x9-inch pan. Bake at 325 degrees for 50 minutes. Serve warm with whipped cream.

Banana Bread

1 cup sugar

⅓ cup butter or vegetable shortening

6 tablespoons buttermilk

2 eggs, beaten

3 small overly ripened bananas, mashed

2½ cups flour, divided

1 teaspoon baking soda

1 teaspoon vanilla

1 teaspoon lemon juice

Pinch salt

In mixing bowl, cream together sugar and butter. Add buttermilk, eggs, and bananas. Add 1 cup flour together with baking soda. Add remaining flour, vanilla, lemon juice, and salt. Grease and flour 1 large loaf pan. Bake at 350 degrees for 45 minutes to 1 hour, testing with toothpick for doneness. Cool for about 5 minutes and remove from pan to rack. If desired, chopped nuts may be added before baking.

Honey Wheat Bread

1½ cups water

1 cup cream-style cottage cheese

½ cup honey

¼ cup butter

6 cups flour

1 cup whole wheat flour

2 tablespoons sugar

2 teaspoons salt

1 egg

2 packages active dry yeast

Extra butter

Heat water, cottage cheese, honey, and butter in medium saucepan until very warm but not boiling. In large bowl, combine 2 cups flour with warm mixture. Add wheat flour, sugar, salt, egg, and yeast. Beat for 2 minutes. By hand, stir in remaining flour to make stiff dough. Knead dough on well-floured surface until smooth and elastic (about 2 minutes). Place in greased bowl. Cover; let rise in warm place until light and doubled in size (45 to 60 minutes). Grease 2 loaf pans with shortening. Punch down dough; divide and shape into 2 loaves. Place in greased pans. Cover; let rise in warm place until doubled in size. Heat oven to 350 degrees. Bake for 40 to 50 minutes until deep golden brown and loaves sound hollow when tapped. Immediately remove from pan. Brush with butter.

Apple Spice Bread

2⅔ cups flour

1½ teaspoons baking soda

1 teaspoon salt

2 teaspoons cinnamon

¼ teaspoon nutmeg

¼ teaspoon ground cloves

2 cups sugar

1 cup vegetable oil

4 eggs, beaten

2 teaspoons vanilla

4 cups chopped apples

1 cup raisins

1 cup chopped pecans

2 teaspoons sugar mixed with
¼ teaspoon cinnamon

Preheat oven to 325 degrees. Grease 2 loaf pans and line bottoms with greased wax paper. In large bowl, combine flour, baking soda, salt, and spices. Set aside. In mixing bowl, combine sugar and oil. Beat in eggs and vanilla. Stir in chopped apples, raisins, and pecans. Add dry ingredients and mix until well blended. Pour batter into pans, smoothing top with spatula. Bake for 20 minutes. Sprinkle loaves with cinnamon-sugar mixture. Continue baking for 30 to 40 minutes or until wooden pick inserted in center comes out clean. Cool for 10 minutes; turn out onto wire rack. Slice and serve.

When we celebrate Christmas, we are celebrating that amazing time when the Word that shouted all the galaxies into being, limited all power, and for the love of us came to us in the powerless body of a human baby.

MADELEINE L'ENGLE

Christmas Sweet Bread

1 cup butter

1 cup sugar

1 cup sorghum syrup

3 teaspoons baking powder

⅛ teaspoon baking soda

¼ teaspoon salt

3 cups flour

4 eggs, beaten

Melt butter in saucepan. Add sugar and syrup. Heat until lukewarm. In separate bowl, mix baking powder, baking soda, and salt with flour. Add to first mixture. Add beaten eggs and mix well. Pour into well-greased oblong pan and bake at 275 degrees until done.

Glazed Blueberry Biscuits

2¼ cups flour, divided

½ cup sugar

1 tablespoon baking powder

½ teaspoon lemon zest

¾ teaspoon salt

¼ teaspoon baking soda

⅓ cup shortening

1 egg, lightly beaten

¾ cup buttermilk

¾ cup frozen blueberries, do not thaw

Topping:

3 tablespoons butter, melted

2 tablespoons sugar

¼ teaspoon cinnamon

Dash nutmeg

In large bowl, mix 2 cups flour with sugar, baking powder, lemon zest, salt, and baking soda. Cut in shortening until mixture resembles coarse crumbs. Mix egg and buttermilk. Stir into flour mixture. Stir in frozen blueberries. Sprinkle remaining flour on countertop. Flour fingers and gently knead dough a few times, just until dough begins to hold together. Pat dough into ½-inch-thick rectangle. Cut with floured 2-inch round cutter. Place biscuits 2 inches apart on lightly greased baking sheet. Bake in center of a preheated 400 degree oven for 12 to 15 minutes, or until lightly browned. Combine topping ingredients and brush over warm biscuits.

Pumpkin Bread

3 cups sugar

3½ cups flour

2 teaspoons baking soda

1½ teaspoons salt

1 teaspoon cinnamon

1 teaspoon ginger

1 cup vegetable oil

4 eggs, beaten

⅔ cup water

1 (16 ounce) can pumpkin

Sift sugar, flour, baking soda, salt, and spices in large mixing bowl. Make well in center of dry ingredients. Add oil, eggs, water, and pumpkin. Blend well; pour into 2 small greased loaf pans. Bake at 325 degrees for 1 hour and 10 minutes.

Pumpkin Pudding

1 (15 ounce) can pumpkin puree
1 tablespoon pumpkin pie spice
2 teaspoons vanilla
1 (12 ounce) can evaporated milk
½ cup sugar

¼ cup brown sugar
½ cup biscuit baking mix
2 tablespoons butter
2 eggs

Spray slow cooker with nonstick spray. Beat all ingredients until smooth in mixing bowl and add to slow cooker. Cook on low for 6 to 8 hours. Serve with whipped topping.

Nutty Caramel Corn

3 quarts popped popcorn

3 cups dry-roasted mixed nuts, unsalted

1 cup brown sugar

½ cup light corn syrup

½ cup butter, no substitutions

½ teaspoon salt

½ teaspoon baking soda

1 teaspoon vanilla

In large roasting pan, combine popcorn and nuts. Place in oven at 250 degrees while preparing glaze. In medium saucepan, combine brown sugar, corn syrup, butter, and salt. Bring to a boil over medium heat, stirring constantly. Continue to boil for 4 minutes without stirring. Remove from heat. Stir in baking soda and vanilla and pour over warm popcorn and nuts. Toss to coat well. Bake at 250 degrees for 1 hour. Stir every 10 minutes. Cool and break apart. Store in airtight container.

Chocolate Truffles

⅔ cup heavy whipping cream
2 cups milk chocolate chips

2 teaspoons vanilla
Chopped nuts or cookie crumbs

In saucepan, heat cream almost to boiling. Remove from heat and add chocolate chips. Whisk gently until chocolate is melted and mixture is smooth. Stir in vanilla and pour into bowl. Cover and refrigerate for 3 hours or until firm. When chocolate mixture is solid enough to work with, scoop into 1-inch balls and roll in finely chopped nuts or cookie crumbs. Place truffles on waxed paper, cover loosely, and chill overnight. Store in tightly covered container.

Creamy Pralines

1¼ cups sugar
¾ cup brown sugar
½ cup evaporated milk

4 tablespoons butter, frozen
1 tablespoon vanilla
1½ cups pecans

In large saucepan, boil sugars and milk until small amount forms soft ball when dropped into very cold water. Remove from heat. Add frozen butter, vanilla, and pecans. Beat until creamy and stiff. Drop onto buttered wax paper. Let cool. Remove from wax paper and store in tightly covered container.

Peanut Brittle

2 cups sugar
1 cup light corn syrup
½ cup water
1 cup butter

2½ cups dry-roasted peanuts, unsalted and warmed
1 teaspoon baking soda
1 teaspoon vanilla

In large saucepan over medium heat, combine sugar, corn syrup, and water. Stir until sugar dissolves. When syrup comes to a boil, blend in butter and stir frequently. Continue cooking until candy thermometer registers 280 degrees. Immediately add peanuts and stir constantly until thermometer reaches 305 degrees. Remove from heat and quickly add baking soda and vanilla, mixing well. Immediately pour into 2 jelly roll pans and spread as closely as possible to edges. When cool, lift from pans using spatula and break into pieces.

Sugared Pecans

1 egg white
1½ teaspoons water
½ teaspoon salt

1 teaspoon cinnamon
¾ cup sugar
½ pound pecan halves

Preheat oven to 300 degrees. With fork, beat egg white and water.
Set aside. Combine salt, cinnamon, and sugar in resealable plastic bag.
Place pecans in egg mixture. Remove with slotted spoon to drain off
extra moisture. Place in bag and shake. Line baking pan with foil and
bake for 30 to 45 minutes, stirring every 15 minutes. Freeze in airtight
container. Will keep for up to two months.

Fudge, candy, and sugared pecans make wonderful Christmas gifts that can be made weeks in advance. Plan to make a few batches right after Thanksgiving and subtract some stress from your December calendar!

Festive Fudge

3 cups sugar

⅔ cup cocoa

Dash salt

1½ cups evaporated milk

4½ tablespoons butter

1 teaspoon vanilla

1 cup chopped walnuts

In large saucepan, blend sugar, cocoa, and salt until all lumps are dissolved. Gradually add evaporated milk and mix well. Put on medium heat and stir often. Let mixture boil up to top of pan and back down. Remove from heat. Add butter and vanilla. Mix well. Add nuts. Beat fudge as it cools until it thickens and loses its gloss. Quickly spread into buttered 9x9-inch pan. Let cool. Cut into squares before fudge is completely cooled.

Peanut Butter Cookies

2½ cups flour
1 teaspoon baking powder
1 teaspoon baking soda
¼ teaspoon salt
1 cup butter

1 cup peanut butter
1 cup sugar
1 cup brown sugar
2 eggs
1 teaspoon vanilla

Stir first 4 ingredients and set aside. Beat butter and peanut butter until smooth. Beat in sugars, eggs, and vanilla. Add flour mixture. If necessary, chill dough. Shape into 1-inch balls and place on ungreased cookie sheet. Bake at 350 degrees for 12 minutes.

Sour Cream Cutouts

¼ cup shortening
¼ cup butter, softened
1 cup sugar
1 egg
1 teaspoon vanilla
2⅔ cups flour

1 teaspoon baking powder
½ teaspoon baking soda
½ teaspoon salt
¼ teaspoon nutmeg
½ cup sour cream

In mixing bowl, cream shortening, butter, sugar, egg, and vanilla. Add flour, baking powder, baking soda, salt, and nutmeg. Gradually add sour cream. Mix well. Roll ¼-inch thick, sprinkle with sugar, and cut with floured cutter. Bake at 425 degrees for 8 to 10 minutes.

And is it true,
This most tremendous tale of all,
Seen in a stained-glass window's hue,
A baby in an ox's stall?
The maker of the stars and sea
Became a child on earth for me?

SIR JOHN BETJEMAN

Old-Fashioned Chocolate Chip Cookies

1⅛ cups sifted flour

¼ teaspoon baking soda

½ teaspoon salt

½ cup shortening

¼ cup brown sugar

½ cup sugar

1 egg, beaten

1½ teaspoons vanilla

½ cup chopped walnuts, if desired

8 ounces semisweet chocolate chips

Sift flour, baking soda, and salt together. Set aside. In mixing bowl, cream shortening and sugars. Add egg and vanilla. Mix thoroughly. Add sifted ingredients. Fold in walnuts and chocolate chips. Drop from teaspoon onto greased baking sheet. Bake at 350 degrees for 8 to 10 minutes.

Recipe Index